What's in this book

This book belongs to

_____

他们说什么语言？
What languages do they speak?

学习内容 Contents

沟通 Communication

说说某人的国籍
Talk about someone's nationality

说说某人会说的语言
Talk about the languages someone speaks

生词 New words

★	中国	China
★	中国人	Chinese (people)
★	英国	the United Kingdom
★	英国人	British
★	美国	the United States
★	美国人	American
★	汉语	Chinese (language)
★	英语	English (language)
★	会	can, to be able to
★	说	to speak

你好

안녕하세요

مرحبا

Hello

Hola

Hallo

こんにちは

привет

Bonjour

Olá

写   to write

国家   country

文化 Cultures

外来词
Loan words

句式 Sentence patterns

你是哪国人?
Which country are you from?

你会不会说英语?
Can you speak English?

跨学科学习 Project

认识世界语言
Learn about world languages

我会说英语和汉语。
I can speak English and Chinese.

Get ready

1   Do you know the languages in the picture?

2   What language do you speak?

3   What language do you want to learn?

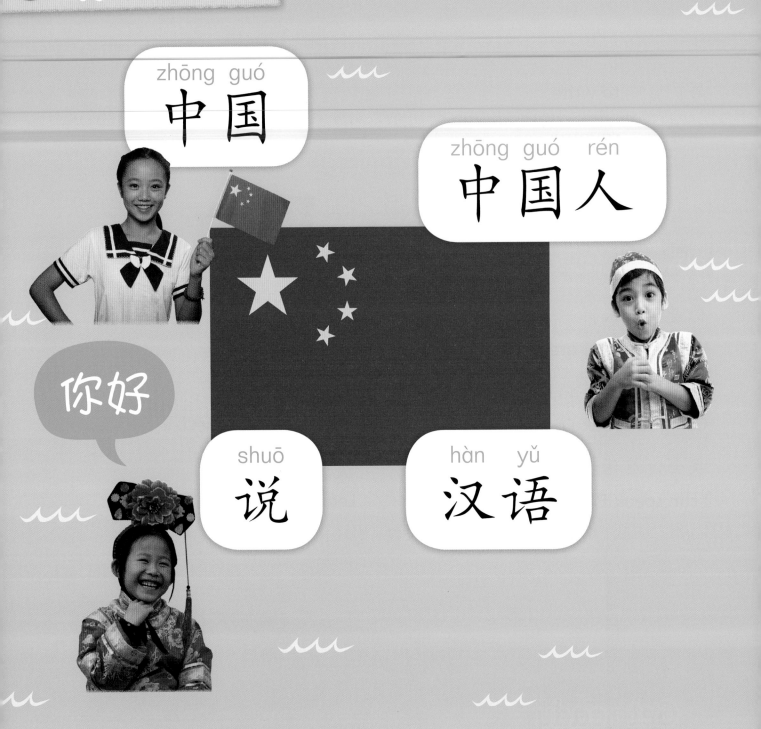

zhōng guó
中国

zhōng guó rén
中国人

你好

shuō
说

hàn yǔ
汉语

我们是中国人，我们说汉语。

yīng guó rén
英国人

yīng guó
英国

yīng yǔ
英语

Hello

我们是英国人，我们说英语。

měi guó rén
美国人

měi guó
美国

Hello

我们是美国人，我们也
说英语。

guó jiā
国家

huì
会

Hello

我们是不同国家的人，
我们都会说英语。

xiě

写

我们也会写一样的文字，
我们都是朋友。

你是哪国人？你会不会
说英语？会不会说汉语？

Let's think

1 Match the countries to the flags.

the United Kingdom 英国   China 中国   the United States 美国

•   •   •

•   •   •

2 Do you know where on the world map are China, the United Kingdom and the United States? Discuss with your friend what you know about these countries.

New words

1 Learn the new words.

英语

English

汉语

会

说

写

国家

中国　中国人　英国　英国人　美国　美国人

2 What nationalities are they? What languages do they speak?
Write the letters.

a 中国人　b 英国人　c 美国人　d 英语　e 汉语

🎧 03 **1** Listen, number and say.

🎧 04 **2** Look at the pictures. Listen to the sto

你好。

① 你会不会说英语？

我会说英语。

②

③ 你是哪国人？

我是英国人。

...d say.

> 你是哪国人？

> 我是中国人。

> 你会不会写？

> 会说汉语，不会写。

3 Write the letters. Role-play with your friend.

a 汉语　b 会不会　c 哪　d 会

1

> 你是＿＿＿＿国人？
> 你＿＿＿＿说英语吗？
> 你喜欢看书吗？

> 我是英国人，我会说英语，我喜欢看书。

2

> 你是中国人吗？
> 你说＿＿＿＿吗？
> 你＿＿＿＿说英语？

> 我是中国人，我会说汉语和英语。

3

> 你是哪国人？
> 你喜欢做什么？
> 你＿＿＿＿说汉语？

> 我是美国人，我喜欢唱歌，我不会说汉语。

Task

Paste a photo of someone you admire in the space below.
Introduce him/her to your friend.

他/她叫……

他/她是……人。

他/她……岁。

他/她会说……

和……

你认识他/她吗？

Paste your photo here.

Game

Listen to your teacher and answer.

英国在哪里？
英国人说英语吗？

中国在这里。
中国人说汉语。

中国在哪里？
中国人说英语吗？

英国在这里。
英国人说英语。

Song

🎧 **Listen and sing.**

Olá

Hola

привет

Hello

Bonjour

Hallo

مرحبا

你好

こんにちは

안녕하세요

我是中国人，

我说汉语。

你是英国人，

你说英语。

他是哪国人？

他说什么语言？

他会不会说汉语？

他会不会说英语？

课堂用语 Classroom language

错了。
Wrong.

为什么？
Why?

1+2=?

题目
Question

写一写 Write

1 Learn and trace the stroke.

横折提

2 Learn the component. Trace ⟨ι⟩ to complete the characters.

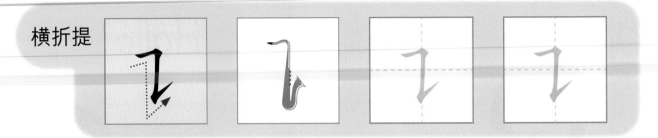

说 语 话 谈

3 Circle the characters with ⟨ι⟩ and say their meanings.

悟 说 射 语

谢 悦 情

谁 准 请

4 Trace and write the character.

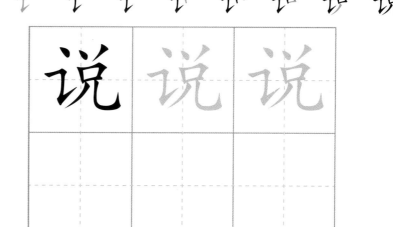

说 说 说

5 Write and say.

我 会 ☐ 英语。

我 会 ☐ 汉语。

汉字小常识 Did you know?

Colour the component that encloses another one red. Colour the top-right component green.

Some characters include a component on all four sides. Other characters include a component that is placed on top and on the right.

 国 回 图 可 句 式

Cultures

1 Languages influence each other. Learn about some loanwords in English and Chinese.

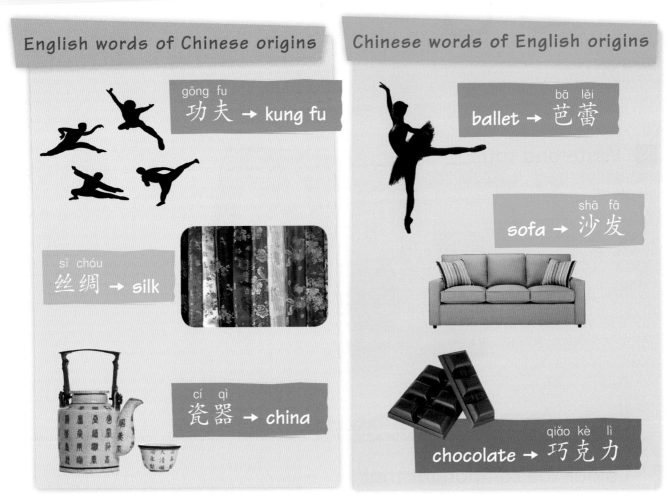

English words of Chinese origins

gōng fu
功夫 → kung fu

sī chóu
丝绸 → silk

cí qì
瓷器 → china

Chinese words of English origins

bā lěi
ballet → 芭蕾

shā fā
sofa → 沙发

qiǎo kè lì
chocolate → 巧克力

2 Practise the pronunciations of some more loanwords.

汉语 → 英语		英语 → 汉语	
tái fēng 台风 ↓ typhoon	lì zhī 荔枝 ↓ lychee	hamburger ↓ hàn bǎo bāo 汉堡包	bus ↓ bā shì 巴士

1 Match and write the letters. Say the names of the countries in Chinese after your teacher.

| a Saudi Arabia | b China | c France | d Germany |

| e Portugal | f Russia | g Spain | h the United Kingdom |

中国 ◯

英国 ◯

法国 ◯

德国 ◯

俄罗斯 ◯

葡萄牙 ◯

西班牙 ◯

沙特阿拉伯 ◯

2 Learn about world languages. In which languages can you greet your friend?

A world language is a language that is spoken internationally and is learnt and spoken by a large number of people as a second language.

Chinese
你好

English
Hello

French
Bonjour

German
Hallo

Spanish
Hola

Russian
привет

Portuguese
Olá

Arabic
مرحبا

温习 Checkpoint

1 Guess who they are. Write the letters and say in Chinese.

a 他不是英国人，他说英语。

b 她不是英国人，她说汉语，也会说英语。

c 她不是美国人，也不是中国人，她说英语。

2 Complete the puzzle.

1				L						
	2			A						
	F	R	E	N	C	H				
P	O	R	T	U	G	U	E	S	E	
		R	U	S	S	I	A	N		
	3			A						
			G	E	R	M	A	N		
4				E						

1   What does 英语 mean?
2   What language do the people in Spain speak?
3   What language do the people from Arab countries speak?
4   What is 汉语 in English?

3 Work with your friend. Colour the stars and the chilies.

Words	说	读	写
中国	☆	☆	🌶
中国人	☆	☆	🌶
英国	☆	☆	🌶
英国人	☆	☆	🌶
美国	☆	☆	🌶
美国人	☆	☆	🌶
汉语	☆	☆	🌶
英语	☆	☆	🌶
会	☆	☆	🌶
说	☆	☆	☆
写	☆	🌶	🌶
国家	☆	🌶	🌶

Words and sentences	说	读	写
你是哪国人？	☆	☆	🌶
我是中国人。	☆	☆	🌶
你会不会说英语？	☆	☆	🌶
我会说英语和汉语。	☆	☆	🌶

Talk about someone's nationality	☆
Talk about the languages someone speaks	☆

4 What does your teacher say?

My teacher says ...

21

分享 Sharing

こんにちは

Words I remember

中国	zhōng guó	China
中国人	zhōng guó rén	Chinese (people)
英国	yīng guó	the United Kingdom
英国人	yīng guó rén	British
美国	měi guó	the United States
美国人	měi guó rén	American
汉语	hàn yǔ	Chinese (language)
英语	yīng yǔ	English (language)

Hallo

привет

Bonjour

你好

Hello

会	huì	can, to be able to
说	shuō	to speak
写	xiě	to write
国家	guó jiā	country

Other words

不同	bù tóng	not the same
都	dōu	all
一样	yī yàng	same
文字	wén zì	writing

Olá

Oxford University Press is a department of the University of Oxford.
It furthers the University's objective of excellence in research, scholarship,
and education by publishing worldwide. Oxford is a registered trade mark of
Oxford University Press in the UK and in certain other countries

Published in Hong Kong by
Oxford University Press (China) Limited
39th Floor, One Kowloon, 1 Wang Yuen Street, Kowloon Bay,
Hong Kong

Illustrated by Anne Lee and Wildman

Photographs for reproduction permitted by Dreamstime.com

China National Publications Import & Export (Group) Corporation is an authorized distributor of
Oxford Elementary Chinese.

Please contact content@cnpiec.com.cn or 86-10-65856782

ISBN: 978-0-19-082196-8

10 9 8 7 6 5 4 3 2